Dr. Mc

Love —

Dorothy's Heart

Book of Poetry

by

Dorothy E. Foster

Bloomington, IN   Milton Keynes, UK
authorHOUSE®

AuthorHouse™
1663 Liberty Drive, Suite 200
Bloomington, IN 47403
www.authorhouse.com
Phone: 1-800-839-8640

AuthorHouse™ UK Ltd.
500 Avebury Boulevard
Central Milton Keynes, MK9 2BE
www.authorhouse.co.uk
Phone: 08001974150

© 2007 Dorothy E. Foster. All rights reserved.

No part of this book may be reproduced, stored in a retrieval system, or transmitted by any means without the written permission of the author.

First published by AuthorHouse 3/15/2007

ISBN: 978-1-4259-8485-4 (sc)

Library of Congress Control Number: 2006911104

Printed in the United States of America
Bloomington, Indiana

This book is printed on acid-free paper.

Dedication

This book was written in dedication to my mother, Sue Fletcher and my daughter, Nicole Burke, as well as to my grandsons (Cameron & Deidrick Burks, Jr) and my siblings.

Special Thanks I offer to my mother who gave me life, to "Barb" (you know who you are), to Lisa Keith and above all to my Heavenly Father who endowed me with the ability, experience and desire to write and share my heart.

"Lost Love"

I Lost Again At Love
Today
I Want to Say "I'm Sorry"
If I May
I Say "Good-bye"
I Will Not Cry
I'll Let You Go
I Make No Fuss
I Will Accept
What Happened Between Us
If I Happen to Cross your Mind
Please Be Kind
I Will think About You Every Now And Then
I Hope and Pray That Some Day
We Both Will Be Able to Love Again

"A Love Gone By"

I Shared A Love With You
A long Time Ago
Back Then
I Did Not Know
A Love So Rare
Oh How you Did Care
Laughter and Joy
All Day Long
My Heart Continuously Sang
This Song
Your Kiss To My Lips
Made My Heart Turn Flips
I Know You Don't Love Me Anymore
Yet, I Stand Here at the Door
I Stand Here With My Heart in Hand
I Know You Can Never Again Be My Man
So I Will Let you Go
You Will Never Know I Loved You So

"I Stayed Too Long At The Fair"

We Both Were Young
Not Old Enough to Understand
What Love Meant; The Divine Plan
I Looked In Your Eyes
You Took My Hand
What I Saw Was a Tall Man
I Remember You Said
It Was Love At First Sight
As I Received Your Smile
My Heart Took Flight
We Traveled Through Life
Without A Care
Because I knew For Me
You Would Always Be There
All of A Sudden
Life Began To Change
Both of Our Hearts
Were Rearranged
When I Look Back Through Our Yesterdays
My Heart Wouldn't Let Go
I Tried to Release You to Love Again
It Was Too Much Pain
In My Heart, You'll Always Remain
I Was Unaware
I Stayed Too Long At The Fair

"Paths"

So If Our Paths Never Cross Again
Down On this Earth, In This Land
I Want You to Know You Are a Great Friend
I'll Never Forget
I'll Always Remember
That Cold Day in November
You Took My Hand
I Felt the Splinter
You Saw What No Other Man Could See
You Loved Me for Me
I Know It's Over
What We Shared
Just Wanted You to Know
I Cared

"You"

*From My Mouth
To God's Ear
In My Heart
I Hold You Near
I Pray For You
Night and Day
So He Can Keep You
In His Face
I Wish peace and Joy
On Your Life
Don't Doubt My Love
Don't Think Twice
I Believe God Has For You
The Very Best
He'll Teach and Keep You
Your Heart He will Test
So Trust In Him
And You Will See
Jesus Our Savior
Who Walked On Water From Galilee*

"Helping You, Lord"

*Jesus, Change Me
Purify My Heart
Help To Cause
Someone to Have A New Start
I Want to Be A Part
Of Your Divine Plan
In Your Name
I Want To Help My Fellow Man
In Every Meeting Or Contact
I Want
To Make A Difference
To Usher In the Plan of Your Great Deliverance
I'll Use My Voice
To Give Someone A Choice
From Wrong To Right
I Will Help Fight
For Life*

"LORD"

The Love You Give
I Can't Live
Without
In My Mind
There is No Doubt
I Live and Breathe
Through Your Love
Pure, Yet Simple
From Up Above
I'll Never Find
A Love So True
You'll Never Leave Me
Feeling Blue
I Trust You Completely
With My Whole Heart
Thank You
Thank You
My Dearest Sweet Lord

"GOD"

*You Prove Your Love For Me
Each and Every Day
By My Side*

You Will Stay
*You Hold My Future
You Have Forgiven My Past
Your Love For Me
I Know Will Last
Someday I will See You
Face to Face
In All of Your Glory
And Divine Grace
What You Did at Calvary
I Can Never Repay
But In My Heart
You Will Always Stay*

"I Trust In You"

I Believe In you
That's How I Do What I Do
In You, I'll Trust
I'll Make No Fuss
On My Journey of Life
You Will Walk Me Through
Carefully Assisting Me
In Every Thing I Do
All of My Hopes and Dreams
Will Come True
Because of A God Like You
I'll Have Love
For My Fellow Man
You Will Find Me
Lending A Helping Hand

"Treasure"

Treasure Is Not
A Pot of Gold at the End of a Rainbow
Treasure Does Not
Live at the Bottom of the Ocean
Treasure
Lives Within You
It Lives Within Me
If You Will Open Your Heart
Find A Place for Your Fellow Man
Across the Ocean
In A Foreign Land
Be Kind to God's Greatest Creation
Man

"Tomorrow"

The Day Before Yesterday

Is A Memory in My Mind

The Day After Today

Is On the Horizon

Today Is Slowly Getting Away

What Will Tomorrow Bring

I Don't Know

I Can Only Dream

"Fall"

As the Leaves Turn
On All of the Trees
This is A Special Time
For Me
A Walk in the Park
I'll Hurry Home Before Dark
A Coat and Some Gloves
A Hat on My Head
A Time to Share
A Time to Be Alone
Seeing the Children Playing
A Crackling Fire
You Will Find Me
With Joy in My Eyes
And
Peace in My Heart

"Christmas"

Green Trees
Bright Lights
Pretty Ornaments Hanging From The Eaves
Pretty Ribbon
Pretty Bows
Tape
Wrapping Paper
Tissue Red and Green
A Little Mistletoe
Everybody Knows
Cold Winter Day
So Brisk and Pure
Santa and his Reindeer
Will So Appear
A Present For You
A Gift From Me
This is My Favorite
Time of Year

"Sky Blue"

Up above in the sky
I see all kind of birds
And fowl that can fly
As I look around I
Imagine sand and
The sea all around me
On the ground a shell…
I think to myself
An oyster must live
There. As I gaze
Across the deep
Blue sea there's
A shadow on the waters…
I see a Lady…I dared
To look closer…
That Lady was me.

"Tree"

I looked out of my stained
Glass window, I see a squirrel…
He's gathering acorns as if
They were precious.
There's a lesson to be
Learned as we travail
Life's journey.

"Rain"

Rain, rain, please go away.
You may return tomorrow.
At this same time of day.

"My Prayer"

Jesus, when will you return?
That's my question,
I hope someday soon to learn.
I pray in the morning time,
I pray at noon.
Lord, please give me a sign
That you will return soon.

"The Letter"

Here's a few lines that crossed my mind…
As you crossed my thoughts today.
I just want to say…
Hope you're having a good day.
I wish you well
As you can tell.
(close eyes)
I am there
Because you
Are in my every prayer.

"My Wedding"

He's here...
I'm here...
As we exchange our rings
We say our vows...
As the choir sings.
The Minister prays
As our journey begins...
We're hoping that our love
Never ends.
Years have gone by...
Our love remains the same.
I still have his heart,
I'm still wearing his name.

"A Soon Coming King"

Children of God, Saints everywhere,
The King of all Kings,
Lord of all Lords.
Jesus Christ will soon appear.
A soon coming King
A soon coming King

He'll wipe every tear, you'll be burden free,
Trust and believe and you will see.
People are looking far and near
For someone to love, someone so dear.
A soon coming King
A soon coming King

Read the word, assemble yourselves, stay prayed up
And humble yourselves. Love one another.
Sing Him praises all the day long,
For we are looking for a better home.
A soon coming King
A soon coming King

Rejoice in your hearts, renew a right spirit,
Prepare to receive a soon coming king.
Read the Word, put on your armor,
Keep your mind stayed on Thee.
For God is righteous and He wants us whole,
For when we leave He wants your soul.
A soon coming King
A soon coming King

A soon coming King
A soon coming King
In Jesus Christ

Mister

I saw him today…
He's in my thoughts,
On my mind.
He hasn't changed from yesterday.

A few gray hairs…
A middle spread…
Still a lot of black…
Hair on his head.

He's unaware of the attention I pay.
Wish I could gain the courage,
There's got to be…
Something I could say.

*He's tall, about six feet
As he stands,
I kid you not,
He's quite a man.*

*He's a dark shade of brown,
His eyes are cold black.
In a blue suit I'd love to see,
I'm dressed in yellow…He's walking
Beside me.*

*This man puts up with no stuff,
His attitude comes off rough.
Hiding behind a half-sized smile,
he's quite a guy,
With a style that will make you smile.*

Thanksgiving Day

Thanksgiving day you knocked on my door,
Who's there? What do you need?
As I turned the knob.
I've always been told…turn no one away
Just might be an angel visiting today.

All that I am
All that is me

Come in…care for coffee or would you prefer tea
Rest yourself…your coat…sit, please stay.
I looked in your eyes, on that cold winter day,
I could almost see a ray of sunshine peep
Through my window, shining my way.

All that I am
All that is me

*You said hello, am I at the right door? Can I sit,
may I stay?
I sipped on coffee, you preferred tea.
I glanced out the window; a daydream was
there…
Glass slippers on my feet,
Me in a yellow dress, you in your finest attire…*

*The dream went away as you stood to say,
This meeting was no accident…
It was you that I sought on this wonderfully cold
day.*

*All that I am
All that is me*

*We said our good byes as our eyes met,
Then we both turned away…
Happy Thanksgiving, he said, that's all I wanted
to say.*

Praises

Here comes another blue Monday
Headed my way.
I asked last night
For a brighter day.

Tomorrow I will praise you
With a new song in my heart
Cause I know everyday
Your mercies are anew
They will give me a new start.

Thank you for the stars and the moon
That light up the sky
For families and friends,
For smiling on my life
Until the day I die.

Forest

*In the forest there are bear trees
Butterflies on the leaves.
As I walk through the forest
There is a cool breeze.*

*All the animals are so friendly
And at peace.
I am reminded of a spring day
Not so long ago.*

*Every animal around was hiding
In the bushes and trees.
They were afraid of me…I finally
Showed myself Friendly.*

*They came out to gaze at me.
They saw that I was Friendly
So they all came out to greet me
We ran, we played, we had a ball.
Fun was finally had by one and all.*

Elbert: A Twin's Homecoming

As I walk through the gateway of Heaven
I always look over my shoulder.
I see all that I have left behind.
Yet I feel no regrets for I know that God has blessed them
To hold on to my memories so I shall not be forgotten,
Your twin sister Evelyn.
I am honored to have been your twin
The bond we share will never end.

Home Is Where Love Is

People always say home is where the heart is, but actually home is where Love is.

Love You Mom
Happy Birthday

God

God is someone you can tell your problems when you can't tell no one else. God is someone you can count on in your time of need. When you have a death in your family and you're feeling sad. He might not can bring them back, but he'll help you get through your time of sorrow. Even though he can't be here in sight, he will always be in our hearts.

Your Smile

*Always keep a smile on your face because you'll never know when
Someone will need it.*

Place In My Heart

There will always be a place for you in my heart if you care for me as much as I do for you.

Your Someone

*You're always someone, if you believe in yourself.
Don't believe in what someone else tells you
Because someone could hurt you for life.*

Love

Love is a word
So widely used
So misunderstood
So so abused
Love is a Word
We all can grab
A word that we all can have
Love is found
In a heart that is true
Love is a word
That we all can share
Love means
That we take time to care

Daughter

A precious little girl
Arrived in this world
A gift for me from God
I give thanks to my Lord
I can never say enough
Nor to show my gratitude
So I will feed her
And change her diapers
I will train her, teach her
Stand by her
Through good times
And through bad
Thank you for this precious gift
From above
Through this act of your kindness
I have to say
That I have experienced
Most precious love

An original poem to my daughter, Nicole
With love, Your Mom

Miz

*A woman all alone
A woman holding her own
She doesn't wait for me
She doesn't wait for you
She's making it for herself
She relies on no one else
If you are a lady alone
Know
That you can make it
Whatever life dishes out
Know
You can take it
You are not alone
We are all over the world
Black, white
Short, tall
Dorothy, Nicole, Terri or Liz
In your honor,
I'll call you "Miz"*

Grandsons

My two grandsons to whom I love
A gift for me from heaven above
Two hearts so dear
Two hearts so pure
From my eye's view
This simple love so true
A song sung in my heart
From day to day
Sometimes for hours
I watch them play
They can be rough
They can be tuff
Two tender hearts so pure
So gentile
Two hearts so pure
All my days
I will truly feel blessed
Two grandsons
Love my heart will possess

Mother

Mother is one person
That is always there
She's concerned about every care
She sees you like no one else
In her eyes you are precious
When people turn their back on you
She will be there
To comfort you
She will always share her love
A gift she received from God above
Understanding I will get no other
I can always count on
My dear mother

Jesus

Jesus died on the cross
To save the world
To claim the loss
He died for you
He died for me
A precious love
For humanity
He'll come again
To claim his own
From this earth
He'll take us home

Angels

*I had a bad day
Today I was unaware
That you were with me
I thought I was alone
I was on my own
I believe that God assigns
An angel to everyone
So when you are in trouble
And think that you are all alone
Remember that you don't have to
Rely on your own
There's an angel aware
To handle every care*

Our Union

I'm your wife
A partner for life
The love we share
Is blessed by Christ
Lord where you lead
We both will follow
For we know you
Hold our tomorrow

Good News

Have you heard the gospel?
Have you heard the good news?
A man named Jesus from Galilee
He walked on water
He calmed the sea
He's coming back
To claim his bride
On a cloud he will ride
A trumpet will blow for the dead and for the live
From his mouth there will be a loud cry
(Come Hither)
To this old world we'll say good-bye
We will be caught up in the air
Jesus Christ
Will meet us there

Heaven

In my mind
I imagine a place
There Jesus and I will meet face to face
On streets of gold
Children will run and play
In this place
I have always been told
No one there will ever grow old
Saints and the angels will sing forever
God I'm told
Is just that clever
A great feast
Will be partaken by everyone
All of this will be shared by God's
One and only
Begotten son

I Search

I search I do not find
Does this mean I'm out of time
I look around I do not see
Yet I feel that you see me
I cry out Loud in my soul
Yet I feel you hear me
Sometime I feel
So all alone
Sometime I feel
I don't belong
Yet your Love
Always reassures me
I must confess
I haven't always
Done my best
Yet I believe
The salvation
Of my soul will
Complete the rest

Marriage

The Bible says
When a man findth
A wife he find a good thing
He gets down on one knee
And offers her a ring
Their love is a union
Blessed by God
He dealt the man
He dealt with his heart
So lady's the search
Is not ours to pursue
It starts with God
He put love in the man's heart
What God ordain
No man can change

Broken Hearted

*How do I piece back together
A broken heart
I don't know
Where to start
I put my all and all
On the line
The more I gave
The more I fell behind
You said your good byes
This is where
Our journey ends
You said that
We should part
As friends
In life people come
People go you say yes
They say no
I hold my heart
In my hand
Here I stand
Alone again*

My Heavenly Father

I have no wings yet
I can fly as far as
I can see there's blue sky
My dreams will soar
So high above because of you
I believe in the power of love
Tomorrow is not promised
Yet today is at hand
All of this fits
In God's divine plan
I'm on a journey
Just passing through
In the end I will see you
You give your love freely
To everyone who
Will receive
And on your name
They will believe

Your Girl

*You're new in town
I haven't seen you around
Can I be your girl
May I share your world
Once we start
Nothing can keep us apart
No man has ever made me
Feel the way that you do
My heart skips a beat
Every time we meet
I laugh I cry
I don't know why
Please tell me
This feeling will never end
I can't
I can't just be your friend
I look in your eyes
I see us together
Tell me this will last forever
Every waken moment
I can only think about you
I hope
I hope this one is true*

May

*May joy and peace
Fill your heart
May the friendships you know
Never part
May you never let anyone
Come between you and God
Because no one on earth
Can fill that void
May life always treat you kind
I hope trouble
Never fills your mind
May you always
Be at your very best
I hope you pass
All of life's every test*

Back in the day

You were my man
Back in the day
There were always
One or two women
In the way
Everywhere we went
We were hand in hand
Everyday you and I had plans
The love we shared
Was bitter yet sweet
We exchanged our love
I thought that was neat
One day you came by
You said you had to go
The love we had
Could be no mo
So with tears in my eyes
I said go, go, go

"I say"

They say
True love cover
A many fault
They also say
A lesson learned
Is a lesson bought
They say one love
Should be shared by two
That I also believe
To be true
They say
You're my future
I think
You're my past
This love between us
Can never last
You see
I don't want you
In my future
Please remain
In my past

"May Love"

May Love
Always find your two hearts together
With God in the Union
It will last forever
With Joy and Laughter
All the day long
May your Hearts
Always sang a happy song
Your Future Together
Let it lie in God's Hand
This union can be broken
By No Man

"Today"

*Today is different from Yesterday
God has allowed Me
To see things in a whole new way
I see Life at its Best
I Know that He will take Care of the Rest
Today, I have a brand new Start
If I will Allow God to do His Part
So to Yesterday
I say Goodbye
Another Door Closed Today
I began a New Today
God
I'll Spend the Day with You*

Index of Poems by Title

Angels 40
A Love Gone By. 2
A Soon Coming King. 20
Back in the day 50
Broken Hearted. 46
Christmas 13
Daughter 35
Elbert: A Twin's Homecoming. 28
Fall. 12
Forest 27
GOD 8
God 30
Good News 42
Grandsons. 37
Heaven 43
Helping You, Lord 6
Home Is Where Love Is. 29
I say 51
I Search. 44

I Stayed Too Long At The Fair *3*
I Trust In You *9*
Jesus *39*
LORD *7*
Lost Love. *1*
Love *34*
Marriage. *45*
May *49*
May Love *52*
Mister. *22*
Miz *36*
Mother *38*
My Heavenly Father *47*
My Prayer *17*
My Wedding *19*
Our Union *41*
Paths. *4*
Place In My Heart. *32*
Praises. *26*
Rain *16*
Sky Blue *14*
Thanksgiving Day *24*

The Letter *18*
Today *53*
Tomorrow *11*
Treasure *10*
Tree *15*
You *5*
Your Girl *48*
Your Smile *31*
Your Someone *33*

About the Author

Dorothy E. Foster is an African American woman from Murfreesboro, TN. She is the mother of one daughter and the grandmother of two sons. Dorothy has worked numerous jobs in various fields for many years, including sales, housekeeping, etc... Though Dorothy has been writing poetry for many years, this is her first published work. This work describes the heart of Dorothy, as the title indicates.